Built From Broken

Lisa Connolly

Independent Publishing Network

ISBN 978-1-0369-0452-4

Author Lisa Connolly

Published by Built from Broken, Aldridge, West Midlands

Printed in the UK

The CIP catalogue record for this book is available from the British Library.

Built From Broken

Index

Introduction to Built From Broken

Poetry of Healing and Empowerment

Built from Broken is not just a collection of poetry—it is the culmination of a journey of survival, self-discovery, and empowerment. Over the years, I've faced unimaginable pain, from a violent relationship in my twenties to a decade of narcissistic abuse that nearly destroyed me. Yet through it all, I found the strength to rebuild my life, piece by piece, rising from the wreckage of those broken years. Now, as a qualified counsellor, recovery support worker, and advocate for domestic violence survivors, I use my story to help others reclaim their lives.

This book is the voice I found along the way; a voice that I now share with you, hoping it might resonate with those who feel trapped in darkness, unsure of the way forward.

Each of the poems in this collection reflects a fragment of my soul, a moment in time when I felt crushed, lost, or silenced. But they also represent the moments when I rose again, found my footing, and reclaimed my life. Built from Broken speaks to the hearts of those who have been battered by life, offering a reminder that even in our most fractured state, we hold the power to rebuild, to reshape ourselves into something stronger and more resilient.

This book was written not just for me, but for anyone who has ever felt broken; for those who need to know that they are not alone in their struggles. It is a testament to the resilience of the human spirit and a reminder that healing, though often painful and slow, is always possible. My poetry reflects the process of healing from the inside out—through every verse, every emotion, every step towards rebuilding.

To my three heartbeats—Alfie, Oliver, and Harriet—thank you for being the light of my life, the rhythm of my heart, and the joy that fills my every day. You inspire me in ways you'll never fully know, pushing me to grow, love deeper, and always strive to be the best version of myself. In the darkest moments, when life felt like it had taken everything, you gave me the strength to keep going. Your love and laughter became my anchor through the storm.

To my amazing mom, Theresa, you are my rock and best friend; the unwavering force that has stood by me no matter what. Your unconditional love and strength have guided me through my darkest times, and I am forever grateful for everything you've done for me.

A special thank you to Jacky and Donna, the remarkable women at WE:ARE (Women's Empowerment and Recovery Educators) who delivered the Freedom Programme for believing in me when I struggled to believe in myself. Your encouragement has been a lifeline, helping me find my voice and the courage to share it.

And to Pat Craven, the creator of the Freedom Programme, thank you for giving women like me a path to walk towards freedom and healing. Your work has truly been life changing.

I'd also like to extend my deepest thanks to MP Jess Phillips, whose tireless work on behalf of domestic violence survivors has inspired and uplifted so many, including myself. Your book Pain to Power inspired me to keep writing, even when the weight of my past threatened to silence me. When you shared my poem Empowering Women online it gave me the confidence to continue sharing my work publicly and, from there, I had the honour of contributing to the University of Birmingham's research project.

I am also grateful and would like show thanks to Professor Caroline Bradbury-Jones and Dr. Lucy Kelsall-Knight at the University of Birmingham for including me in their research project, which explored, using artwork, how women resist and survive abuse. Their work looks at how women living under regimes of power and control find ways to honour resistance, manage risk, avoid abuse, and cope with pain through creative expression. Contributing my poetry to this project was an honour, and I hope it helps amplify the voices of survivors.

Built from Broken is my story, but it's also a shared experience. So many of us are living through pain, trauma, or loss, but I want to remind you that there is light on the other side. If these poems offer even a glimmer of hope or validation to just one person, then I know that sharing them has been worth it. You are not alone, and your story is far from over.

Every scar you carry is a symbol of strength, and each step you take forward is a victory over the darkness that once held you back. You are not defined by your past but by the courage you show in building your future. Thank you for joining me on this journey.

Now, as a qualified counsellor, recovery support worker, coach, and workshop facilitator, as well as the founder of Built from Broken, I use my journey to empower others in reclaiming their lives. Through my work, I provide counselling, coaching, and support to survivors, partnering with charities that reflect my commitment to meaningful change. My goal is to uplift those who have endured the traumas I once faced, helping them find their strength and their voice.

This book represents the voice I found on my path to healing—a voice I now share with you. I hope its message reaches those who feel lost in darkness, offering a sense of hope and a way forward.

The Healing Healer

I am there for others every day,

Helping them to heal,

In their own way.

I listen deeply,

Create the space,

To work through their feelings at their own pace.

Some struggle to sit in the chair;

No pressure, just calm, my presence is there,

Working within modalities ethical and kind,

Tailoring the journey to each mind.

I love being a counsellor, doing the work I do;

I find joy in helping others to heal and push through;

Yet I know to give my best, I must invest,

In my own self-care, in moments of rest.

Even counsellors need time to renew,

To find time to recharge and value,

To share our thoughts, our fears, our day,

To reflect, restore, and find our way.

I take time for me, to make myself whole,

Finding the space to bring peace to my soul.

Most know not to enquire about my day;

There's a lot I hold, none of which I can say;

But it's a path I've chosen, and here I'll stay.

With the work I do, the heart I give,

I'm reminded, I too must live,

And though I guide others, I too am healing.

For this is not a one-way street, it's a journey we are all feeling.

Embracing the Energy

Breathe in deeply, feel the energy around you,
You're wrapped in light, love, endless possibilities too.
Let it flow through your spirit, soft as the breeze,
As you stand tall with power, so effortlessly at ease.
You are more powerful than you realise,
The strength, the beauty, all rests in your eyes.
Everything you need, already in your soul,
Tap into your energy, let it make you feel whole.
The universe is working, all in your favour;
Trust in the journey, let go and savour.
Abundance is near, just trust and believe,
Embrace the path and you'll achieve.
Today, you are unstoppable, shining so bright,
Your energy lifting others, filling them with light.
Rise, and let the world feel your glow,
Let your inner light guide you wherever you go.
Breathe in the peace, let go of the strain,
Feel the warmth of the sun through the rain.
The universe whispers, its message so clear,
You're exactly where you need to be, no need to fear.
Step into your power, let it carry you high,
Wings of intention will help you to fly.
Every challenge, a gift, a lesson, a guide,
Let your heart be open, let the universe provide.
You are limitless, boundless, full of grace,
Moving forward at your own perfect pace.

Embrace each moment, let love lead the way,

For today is your canvas, and you are the day.

With every breath, your spirit will rise,

Like the stars lighting up the skies.

This is your time, your soul's gentle call,

To shine without limits, to give it your all!

When the Love Bombing Ends

A perfect match,

I was love bombed to hell;

It's the best feeling ever, can everyone tell?!

'I love you so much,

But let's take it slow',

Was a challenge to him even more so.

This stage right here was not real;

Love bombing continued,

Until he sealed the deal.

A union of two that did not grow,

Because, after all,

It was all for show.

Every row you got your own way;

You'd threaten your life;

I'd apologise and stay.

Every time my friends hoped to catch up,

You'd think of ways to screw it up;

You always caused a lot of stress,

Making sure I didn't go,

Seeing my friends less and less.

Isolation grew before I knew it,

No one around, no one to visit,

All the while, with no one knowing,

At home, just us, with me tip toeing.

The Jailer

If you don't answer the phone

I will destroy you.

I hate you.

You b**** where are you?!

Tracking every move,

I'm watching and listening too;

Always keeping a close eye,

To see what you're up to.

I'll lock her out;

I'll not answer the door;

When she comes home,

She can stand outside like a w****.

She calls her mom and gets upset;

"Theresa my key's in the door, how could I forget?

I'm sorry I was sleeping"

My mask is back on...

I'm back to being nice;

She's sorry;

I win,

And I'm number one.

“I love you” he said

Making excuses; covering up the bruises.

Is this love?

Surely, he wouldn’t do this if it was.

He’s so sorry, even soft, warm and loving,

When I have something that needs covering up.

I wish he was this nice all the time,

And cared about the scars that’s left on my mind.

Maybe one day could we leave all this behind?

Oh… my heart…

Why am I constantly treading on eggshells?

I wish I could go back to the start…

Would I walk away?

Or go through it all over again?

And still stay…

I’d try my best!

But maybe this is his way,

Another black eye…

Another apology to get me to lie.

Is this what I deserve?

If it’s that bad, then why can’t I say goodbye?

What would even happen to me to even try?

Another battle to be fought;

If I’m standing at the door with my bags and caught,

I’m scared of what he’d do;

He said “no one’s ever going to love you the way I do”.

If this keeps getting worse, one day I’ll be dead.

But "I love you" he said.

Broken Down to Nothing

Who am I?

I can't understand why;

The times I've been on the floor, wanting to die.

You said you loved me;

The strong person you met,

Was broken down to nothing,

Constantly causing upset.

What did you see when you looked at me?

All I wanted was for us to be.

The names you'd call me shattered me from within;

Anyone would think I'd committed some deadly sin!

I was there for you in every way;

If you didn't like me all along, why didn't you say?

At first, it was good,

But then the red flags waved;

All confidence gone and I completely caved.

Too Scared to Sleep

I won't sleep in my bed;
I can't face the night;
The memories choke me;
The shadows bite.
The dark plays tricks on me,
Panic, fear and dread, everywhere;
Triggers hit fast,
Trapped in the glare.
I finally crash on the settee, half conscious awake;
Kicking and screaming
Nightmares won't let me breathe.
I fight off sleep like you wouldn't believe.
Every creak a threat; every sound a knife;
Tension fills the air, every second of my life.
Stuck in this hell, where the night never quits;
Too shattered to heal, too raw to fix.
Eyes wide open till dawn breaks through the sky;
Just surviving, on the edge, but don't seem to know why.
So, I'll stay on the settee,
Guarding safety,
In hope,
That one day I'll find the strength to truly cope.

Narcissistic Fog

Living in fog, I thought it was just me;

Survival mode before I could see.

I thought it was marriage, but it was not;

The abuse felt like I had been emotionally shot.

Drained of my life, my heart pouring out too;

So much had gone on, I didn't know what to do.

My sense of self I'd just lost touch;

A gaping hole of a soul that's crushed. How could I not see clearly?

I am so ashamed to tell my family...

Living in fog was like being in a trance;

I could hardly breathe, and I could not dance.

Awarded only when he was in a good mood;

I thought it was love,

I craved awards,

Like food.

Unseen Battles

A silent ache; a constant strain;

The simplest of tasks now touched by pain.

Each day unravels its own silent fight;

The unseen battle that tests my might.

The world moves on at a steady pace,

While I sit privately saving some face.

Taken for granted, the past with ease,

Now demands my efforts bringing me to my knees.

Behind a composed smile, there lies a heavy truth,

A daily struggle that robs me of my youth.

Every step I take, every moment I face,

Is a testament of resilience:

A hidden grace.

I am yearning for freedom that I once knew,

When movements were fluid, and my spirit flew;

Now most journeys need a guiding hand,

Pushing despite my body's command.

A body once strong now fights to keep,

The promises it made, the dreams I seek.

This newfound norm is hard to embrace,

A much slower pace, in a darkened place.

I wish for the days where I could roam free,

But for now, I tread more cautiously.

No Way Out

Here in the abyss with no way out,

All I want to do is scream and shout.

I can't find the strength to walk out the door;

He said we're trying… but I've heard it before…

He makes me beg for money for food,

As if I'm a beggar coming in to intrude.

I feel so small when he is around…

I wish I could leave without making a sound.

Here, I'm trapped with nowhere to go;

He's got photos and videos he'd be sure to show.

If we break up it's got to be his choice,

And I know until then,

I have no voice.

Built From Broken

I gave you the key and wanted your love;
I felt so lucky like you'd been sent from above.
Rose-tinted glasses, I was living a lie.
When it became clear what you were doing, I wanted to die.
My broken soul left shattered on the floor;
A bottle of gin in and a head so sore.
Discarded for another where do I begin?
I was left in pain, trauma bonded therein.
Gas lighted for years like I was going insane;
I thought it was love but only myself to blame.
Scared, alone, craving you like air,
Then the realisation that you enjoyed my despair.
Newfound energy to pick up what was broken;
Other survivors were my true gifted token.
Positivity surrounded me as it always should.
Since you left there has been nothing but good!

Triggered

An innocent tap on the shoulder and I jump out of my skin;

Dread sweeps over me, a storm brewing within.

Memories flash like a bolt of lightning;

Cutting through the calm,

Haunting echoes of the past;

A dissonant alarm;

Will it always be this way?

My heart races wildly;

Breath caught in my throat;

Lost in this moment, adrift and remote.

But I breathe through the fear, let the chaos subside,

Finding strength in the struggle, my courage as my guide.

Will I ever lead a normal life?

Will I ever be normal?

Free from this strife?

With each wave of panic, I learn to endure;

Navigating shadows, searching for the cure.

Though the night terrors may linger, and anxiety looms,

I rise from the darkness, pushing through all the gloom and doom.

In the depths of the chaos, I'll find my own way,

Breathing through the fear, I reclaim every day.

Halfway Better

I'm halfway there,

But still on the settee;

It's not perfect,

But it's better for me.

Nightmares still knock,

Even a year on;

I long for the days when they're all gone.

They still creep in at night, but at least now they don't stay,

I fight them off before they take me away.

I feel the shift, not quite free,

But the weight is a little lighter inside of me.

The clouds are parting slightly, but shadows remain;

Each day I grow stronger, shedding the pain.

The beds still waiting, but not tonight;

I'm getting there, I'm just holding on tight.

Freedom

The sun shined brightly within my soul once more;

I did not know it was possible until you walked out of the door.

My life in the shadows became a memory;

As soon as I made sure you were no longer allowed near me,

The possibilities were endless the breath of fresh air,

The freedom I had and no longer despair.

A new lease of life, joyous and exciting too;

I am so much happier now I am no longer with you.

Save Yourself

Knights in shining armour;
Princesses waiting to be saved;
We all believed in fairy tales,
Not a story of us enslaved.
Broken down to nothing;
Scrutinised each day,
Where's my so-called loving Prince gone?
Has he lost his way?
We see the best in others; it comes so easily;
Now take a look in the mirror right now and say,
"It's him who doesn't deserve me!"
We all need saving sometimes,
But let me tell you this,
You cannot turn a frog or a toad even with a true loves kiss.
Women save themselves every day.
We are capable of so much;
Not little beings less than,
Completely out of touch.
So, start a new beginning with this,
We all deserve anew,
I will save myself from this today,
Not be dependant if I fit into a shoe.

Fresh Start

I had to throw myself into being okay.

I wasn't of course but it was the only way.

Keeping busy; learning how to function.

My fresh start when I got an injunction!

I learnt how to breathe and follow my heart,

Do all the things I'd wanted from the start.

Suddenly my world was full of choices.

It felt so strange only hearing positive voices.

Save the Day

If you pluck away at the petals of a flower and stepped on it for years,

It still has a chance at living and growing,

It doesn't fall down in tears.

Our true definition isn't what happens to us,

It's our choice of how we respond,

The way we choose to keep going.

We create our next chapter and beyond;

So, pick yourself up off the floor;

Makes plans with loved ones once more,

A coffee or two, or cheeky gins,

Or go to church and sing a few hymns.

Tomorrow is not promised for all,

But choose to live life today.

Life is really a precious gift, and you can save the day!

Empowering Women

I look, I see,

My reflection,

Staring back at me,

A brave soul,

For all to see;

Standing tall,

Speaking my truth,

Even if the aftermath,

Can be somewhat uncouth;

Handing out blow torches,

To those left in the dark;

Afraid to speak out,

Or seek a future to embark.

I'm on a mission;

I'll plant the seed;

I'm here for the cause,

For all those in need.

I need no applause,

It's not that in which I seek;

I'm reaching my hand out to the others,

And allowing them to speak,

Understanding why it's all hidden,

Because I know only too well,

That my truth was forbidden.

The Aftermath of the Smear Campaign

The abuser surrounded by enablers of abuse,
All insisting that it was me,
Who abused the abuser,
Broke him down and left him empty,
A premeditated and manipulated situation,
Just please leave me be!
Struggling to regulate all the emotions,
That are trapped inside of me;
Up to my neck in everything;
Feeling mental exhaustion too.
Life in full blown overwhelm;
On my knees praying for what I should do.
The extremity of all the lies,
Cut deeper than a double-edged sword,
For most of his family and friends were mine too,
And to think that they were all fully on board,
Walking around all happy;
Elevated that you caused me so much despair;
Taking every penny that we had to buy our house -
How is that even fair?

The Courtroom Smear Campaign

In the storm of all the lies,
And the deceit that they spun,
The smear campaign,
The damage done.
Through the muck and the mud,
I powered through strong,
For the truth was my shield all along.
In the courtroom's glare,
With courage held high,
The allegations false,
But I'd never comply;
The twisted narrative,
His attempts to deceive,
But justice prevailed,
Their web we unweaved.
Proven wrong, the accusations mis-sold;
The truth in my favour, my story to be told.
His plans for discard manipulation sown,
But I emerged resilient and not alone.
He sought to blame, to shift the weight,
But truth couldn't be swayed by a twisted fate.
In the face of darkness, I found my way,
A survivor's strength to face the day.
No longer bound by his hurtful design,
I reclaimed my life, my work, what's mine.
From the ashes of deceit, I rose above,

A testament to resilience, a story of self-love.

Whispering Hope

In the shadows a broken soul stood -
Through tears and pain, so misunderstood –
The past, a darkness, too hard to bear,
Yet, within all that pain, strength was there.
Her sense of self, lost and betrayed;
Invisible scars so deeply laid.
A survivor's strength, a soul's reprise,
Out from the abyss a phoenix flies.
In the silence, a voice emerged,
A tale of courage, now to be heard;
Breaking free from the chains of fear,
Whispering hope,
The heart draws near.
For in the journey there is light,
Guiding through the darkest night;
Healing hands and loves embrace,
A path to peace, a safer place.
Wounds can mend,
A wounded heart can still transcend;
From the pain of yesterday, she finds release,
A chance for love,
For inner peace.

Haunting Truths

Once a year, they rise from the shadows and our fears,
Monsters roam free, fuelled by laughter and cheers.
But beneath the masks, there's a truth that must be seen,
The real ones are lurking, and they're not just for Halloween.
Social angels, charming, with smiles that deceive;
The truth behind closed doors, the devil takes its leave.
They hide amongst us in plain sight, in homes built on dread,
Where love turns to fear, and any hope of comfort is dead.
They wear their masks very well, play the perfect role,
But in the darkness, what's inside of them is a threat to the soul.
It's not just at night, it's a cycle that spins,
In the privacy of homes is where the horror begins.
So, while the world celebrates with costumes and fright,
Just remember that there are monsters in real life,
Who hide amongst us in plain sight.
So, this Halloween, as the shadows take flight,
Let's honour the stories hidden away from the light.
Together we'll all rise, shine a truth that's so bright,
For the monsters who linger will soon fade out of sight.

New Beginnings

I've moved house now,

It all feels like a dream;

Sleeping in my own bed feeling like a sun beam.

Viewing the house, my mom and I cried;

It's just what we needed,

A sanctuary for us to reside.

Family is now close,

The smear campaign at bay;

Quality time as a family,

We laugh;

We joke;

We play.

Even the walls feel like a comfort,

A long-awaited relieved sigh;

I'm safe in this place,

Now my tears can run dry.

The Power of Forgiving – Yourself

Forgiveness isn't weakness, it's a gift to the heart;

In the freedom of letting go, I make a new start.

Over lethal burdens that I've held on to for so long,

In the strength of my healing, I learnt to be strong.

It's the acceptance, the love for the soul;

Each step I take, I'm in full control,

Forgiving myself for not knowing, now I take the reins,

With newfound strength, I break free from the chains.

I carried burdens for years, far too long,

But now I rise, I am strong.

Like a tree shedding its leaves to start anew,

I let go of the past, so the future shines through.

In the mirror, I saw the truth, at last,

The shadows I carried were meant to cast.

I rise from the ashes of pain and despair,

No longer bound by the scars I wear;

Forgiving myself, I reclaim my own light;

Free and empowered, I soar to new heights,

And with courage ignited, I embrace what's in sight.

The Power of Your Voice

There's strength in sharing,

In letting your truth be shown;

When you speak,

You create space,

So no one feels alone.

The silence that binds us,

Won't hold us forever;

In vulnerability,

We find threads,

That bind us together.

We heal;

Your pain isn't a weakness,

It's proof that you feel.

Your story could be,

Someone's guide out of mistakes,

Keep using your voice,

Don't give up the fight;

Every word you release,

Is a step toward the light.

So don't fear,

Speaking up,

Or breaking the chain;

In sharing your truth,

You'll find strength,

To rise again.

Thank you for Saving Me

I knew deep down what I lived through was wrong;
I couldn't see it fully; I couldn't stay strong.
Trapped in the cycle, thinking it was just me;
Trusting my mind, it made it hard to see.
Then the lovely ladies at the freedom programme saw me walk in,
A shadow of myself the first time I came;
With wisdom and grace, helping me to reclaim.
Through every session, each word that you spoke,
The chains of my past fell away like dust and the grip finally broke.
You opened my eyes gave me back my voice;
Taught me that owning my life, was not just a choice, but a right.
A power, a lifeline to hold,
Your guidance and warmth when the world felt so cold.
You saved my life without a shadow of a doubt,
With those quiet truths,
Showing me the way out,
For that I'm forever grateful and I'm forever free;
Thank you for never stopping believing in me.
In your empowering strength, I found my own;
In your light, I've truly grown.
So here's to the freedom programme for the freedom you helped me reclaim;
Thank you for saving me,
I will never be the same.

WE:ARE Warrior Women

We are warrior women, fierce and strong,
Bound by our stories where we all belong.
In circles of courage, we gather and grow,
Reclaiming our power, letting our true selves show.
Each journey is different, yet we all share dread,
A history of battles, a weight of shame we've all fed.
But in shared voices, we start to heal,
And in the warmth of our connections our truth reveals,
We've stared down the darkness;
Weathered the storm;
In the depths of despair;
We've learned to transform,
From silence to strength, pain to power,
More to say with every passing hour.
And in the blaze of sisterhood, we've shattered the dark,
Reigniting our spark,
Rising from the ashes, like a phoenix we soar;
Breaking the chains that bound us before.
With every scar, we became something new,
Warrior women, strong, bold and true.
In these spaces of trust, we find our own way,
Rebuilding our futures from the struggles of today,
Not defined by what's happened before,
We're warriors of change,
Making sure there's no more.
So, let's all stand tall, our hearts open and free,

Warrior women embracing our destiny.

The Freedom Programme

In the heart of The Freedom Programme, we rise,
Breaking the silence, cutting the ties;
A journey of empowerment through knowledge,
Seeing with our 'Freedom Eyes'.
Through workshops and sharing,
We learn to see through their disguise;
Feeling empowered together, standing side by side, we rise.
In this safe space of healing, our spirits collide,
From fear to empowerment, we journey anew,
Finding our voices, reclaiming what's true.
With new skills we learn to reclaim,
Our lives, our future,
We're no longer the same.
We challenge the patterns that once held us tight,
In the glow of our courage,
Away from the fight.
The Freedom Programme shows us the way to build,
A foundation where we all can thrive,
Safe and protected in the guild;
For we are all more than just survivors,
We are warriors of change,
With a mosaic of sisterhood.
Nothing no longer feels strange;
So, here's to our journeys, the battles we've won;
Warrior women united with strength to overcome!

The Gift of Giving Back

In rooms filled with purpose, my spirit ignites,
Engaging with causes that fuel my light.
Passion flows freely, like rivers in spring,
Feeling the connection in all that it brings.
Recognising the energy, reflecting on my path,
Each moment, my way of giving back.
For each act of kindness is my heart's sweet track;
Hope twinkling brightly like the starry night sky,
Through laughter and play, as time goes by.
I see their pain as it mirrors my own;
Through guiding their path, I see my strength has grown.
In each story shared, in each tear that falls,
I witness their rise as they answer the call.
Together we heal, finding courage anew,
For in helping them, I find healing too.

The Art of Healing

We are moving forward, creating anew;
Together we rise and push through;
Community surrounds me, my saving grace,
Feeling the warmth of connection, I found my place.
Through creative arts and poetry, my soul's pure release;
In every word and creation, I found peace.
In crafting and sharing I learned to let go,
Transforming my pain into something to show.
Each stroke of the brush; each line that I write,
Guides me through the darkness and into the light.
Together, we gather, our stories unfold,
In the bonds of our hearts, we find the strength to be bold.
Embracing our journey, new paths that we've made;
One step at a time;
Patience deeply laid.
From ashes to blossoms, we take back our voice;
On our journey to healing we celebrate our choice.
With courage and kindness, we stand side by side;
Feeling empowered, we'll no longer hide.
Together we flourish, our spirits take flight;
In the light of our story, we shine ever bright.

Free to be me

Deep within the mirror's reflection,
I could finally see,
A newfound appreciation for myself,
Unconditionally free.
I have made a choice -
A promise to me -
To keep my essence -
To let it be.
No more dating,
For the sake of being;
I will only allow what is truly freeing.
Boundaries set;
Fortress strong;
Protecting the peace,
I have yearned for,
For so long.
I will not let anyone reshape my soul;
I am complete;
I am whole.
For stability's sake,
For my children's grace,
I will keep to my path in this sacred space.
No more attachments that bring me down;
In my newfound strength,
I will not drown;
I have learnt to cherish -

In my own company -

Finding joy,

In simply being me.

With self-love as my guide,

I embrace my fate;

Each step forward,

I celebrate.

With open arms, I face,

Each dawn of a new day;

No shadows may linger;

No doubts to sway.

I claim my truth,

In the light of the sun;

A journey embraced,

A new life begun.

So here I stand,

Unwaveringly free,

Loving myself,

As I was meant to be.

No more changes;

No more pretence;

I will live life fully,

In my own defence.

Mosaic of Strength

From the shattered pieces, a spirit arose,
Built from broken where courage flows.
Through trials and tribulations untold,
A story of strength, resilient and bold.
In the darkness of trauma's embrace,
A journey began, a daunting chase;
But deep within a fire burnt bright,
A will to survive to reach the light.
With each step forward, a battle was won;
Though the path was tough, I carried on.
Scars may remain, reminders of pain,
They don't define me, they're not my chain.
Through therapy's guidance and healing grace,
I learnt to heal, to feel safe in this place,
To rise above what was confined,
Reclaiming my soul, my spirit, my home, my mind.
No longer defined by the past's cruel hand,
A warrior strong, I'll take my stand.
Built from broken, I've found my way,
To brighter tomorrows, a brand-new day.
With every tear and every fall,
I've learnt to rise; I've learnt to stand tall.
Now I walk with purpose, no longer in fear;
My path is clear, my heart sincere.
With love as my beacon, and love as my guide,
I'll face the future with nothing to hide.

In the quiet of my mind's reflection, I've come to see,

The essence of my spirit, the truth of who I can be.

With each step forward, the mirror reveals,

A self-embraced, with hope of wounds to heal.

Each challenge faced; a lesson learnt;

From every hardship, strength has burnt.

In the darkest moments, I found my light,

And turned the shadows into insight.

With scars as reminders of battles fought,

I've embraced the journey, lessons taught.

What once felt heavy, now feels light,

Forged in the fire, my spirit ignites.

The journey unveiled the soul beneath the mask,

A blend of dreams, hopes and endless tasks.

I've embraced my flaws, my strength, my grace,

Finding beauty in my unguarded place.

Now, as I stand in the light of my design,

I see a heart, unbound, forever free and fine.

Embracing my truth, I am finally whole,

To live in the fullness of a free and vibrant soul.

I don't Owe You Forgiveness

I don't owe you forgiveness; I won't pretend that it's all fine;

You don't deserve a single thought or any peace of mind.

You left; you walked away like nothing ever broke;

While I carried on alone, while you laughed like it was a joke.

I forgive myself for being too kind, for trusting too much;

For being too blind, but you, you stay right where you are,

Beneath the mess, I rise above, you've lost your hold no less;

You can sit with your shadows, no longer with mine;

The weight you left behind, I shed in time.

I rose while you remained in your disguise,

No longer fooled by the lies in your eyes.

I won't chase closure, it's not yours to give,

I've found my peace in learning how to live.

So, stay with your secrets, all buried in deceit,

While I walk around free on stronger feet.

I'm done with the games, the ones you played;

The damage you left; the price I paid.

I've let go of bitterness, it's all yours to keep;

One day you will wrestle with the darkness, while I sleep.

I don't owe you forgiveness, nor a second chance;

I've built my strength; I've remembered how to dance.

Stay beneath the rubble of bridges that you burned;

I'll walk ahead, with the lessons I've learnt.

I've healed the wounds and turned them to gold,

Helping survivors unleash their stories untold.

With every step, I'm now brave and bold;

Stay with your burdens, where you belong,

While I move forward in life singing my own song.

Happy Hermit

I used to be a people person,

But then people ruined it;

Now I am a happy hermit,

Where solitude's a better fit.

I used to be a people person,

But then people broke my trust;

Now I've established boundaries,

And that is a must.

I used to be a people person,

But then people tore me apart;

Now I seek peace while trying to heal my heart.

I used to be a people person,

But then people left me scarred;

Now I'm sheltered in my sanctuary where life doesn't seem so hard.

I used to be a people person,

But then people kept crossing the line;

Now I've embraced stillness,

And silence feels divine.

I used to be a people person,

But then judgements felt too real;

Now I honour my own voice and have learnt to truly heal.

I used to be a people person,

But then chaos brought me pain;

Now I dance with my own shadows and find joy in the rain.

I used to be a people person,

But their dramas would drain my energy thin;

Now I cultivate my garden and only let certain people in.

I used to be a people person,

But now I cherish me;

In the quiet of my sanctuary, I've finally been set free.

So, here's to the happy hermits, who have found comfort in retreat;

In the beauty of solitude, my spirit feels complete.

With every moment cherished, I embrace who I am;

In the stillness, I discover a life that feels like a grand slam.

I used to be a people person,

But now I cherish me;

In this journey of self-love and discovery,

I'm finally truly free to be me.

Shattered Dreams and Rising from the Ashes

Where dreams once were,
Soon torn apart;
Clutching on with a battered heart.
The storm of lies,
Left their mark;
Manipulation of finances,
While kept in the dark.
Three hundred and fifty thousand,
Was all the money we had;
Choosing to leave with every penny;
Twisting narratives to make me look bad.
Sinister motives echoed through each night,
While I faced each dawn without any light.
Your cruelty spread,
Leaving nothing behind;
But still, I fought,
For the peace I'd later find.
Even when I was shattered and torn apart,
I held on fiercely to my fragile heart.
You thought I'd crumble,
Hoped I'd break,
But you never knew,
The fortitude I'd awake.
While searching for foodbanks,
To keep the house afloat,
You flaunted holidays,

Proud to gloat;

Showing off a temporary life,

Like a trophy you'd won,

While I battled alone,

Dealing with what was undone.

I had no escape,

No break from the pain,

But I swore to myself,

That I'd rise up again.

Dignity stripped;

My soul laid bare;

Hoping for a fresh start,

A new home, somewhere;

Questioning who I was in every way,

If there was ever going to be the hope of a brighter day.

But still, in the silence,

Something deep inside,

Whispered that I'd make it,

I'd survive.

From the ashes,

I found my voice,

And my fire.

Lifting my vibrational frequency higher,

I was no longer the woman you left behind;

I reclaimed my soul,

My peace of mind.

Every scar later became a part of my crown;

I was no longer the one you had left to drown.

Raising boys to be better men;
A girl to be strong,
I found that my crown was with me all along.
Keeping busy with my little heart beats,
While breaking inside;
Facing everyone with nowhere to hide;
I wore my pain like a secret cloak;
I never let it publicly suffocate or choke,
For I knew there was more,
Than this shadow of shame;
There was a fire burning,
One you could not tame.
You tried to break me,
Causing my life so much pain;
Only me trusting in you was to blame.
Having my loved ones around me saved my life;
In truth, it was the ending of me as I knew it, becoming your wife.
From ashes of pain, I rebuilt anew;
My loved one's support gave me the strength to push through.
You tried to regain control,
To twist what you could,
But I had found my freedom,
I understood.
Amongst the ashes,
I began to dry my eyes;
Feeling the power from within to my surprise.
Prayers answered,
Within all of the pain,

Was my chance to rebuild and sustain.

Finding inner strength,

The ability to rise and finally see,

Through a new lens,

Of what I wanted to be.

I rebuilt my life,

Piece by piece,

Finding a new home,

And a brand-new lease;

Moving past the lies;

The hurt;

The deceit;

My home became my sanctuary.

A new place to retreat,

A new house;

A new path;

A fresh start;

Pouring my heart and soul into every part.

My children laugh, thrive and play,

And finally, I can say,

That I am proud of the woman I am today.

I reclaimed my story,

I wrote it anew;

I am no longer bound by what you put me through.

I graduated with my first degree;

I stood tall,

Exhilaratingly free;

With the strength regained,

Standing in grace;

No longer haunted by that darkened place.

I didn't just return home,

But to my roots, you see;

I returned to the person,

I was always meant to be.

A Light in the Darkness

I see you in the darkness,

A place I've wandered too;

Where negativity whispers,

And hope feels far from view.

I've walked those miles many times before,

Through trials and trauma deep with pain,

And now I'm here for you,

So, you can heal again.

I know the weight that you are carrying,

The burden that is the past;

Please trust me as we journey,

All this darkness doesn't need to last.

For I found the sunlight,

Beyond the walls of fear;

I'll be here right beside you,

To hold your hand my dear.

Every tear you shed, I will honour;

Every word you speak, I will deeply hear;

In the silence of your heart,

I will guide and help dispel your fear.

Together, we will embark on finding freedom,

A path to brighter days,

Where joy replaces sorrow,

And light renews your ways.

So, trust the steps we are taking,

Though the road ahead seems long,

For I am here to guide you to where you can belong.

Carving a Path

I keep moving forward,

Never slowing my pace;

Three little birds light up my face.

From nothing, I've built what we now call home;

Every job, every project, I do it alone.

We've faced more than our fair share of trials,

From moving house to new survival styles.

Everything we built for ten years,

Was torn apart yet, I fought through the tears;

Fear of the past lingers in my mind,

Days of empty pockets stay left behind.

But I've started over, built it anew;

Proving to myself exactly what I can do.

Multiple jobs I juggle; no time for rest;

Doing the work of many; giving it my best.

Each task I tackle with unwavering grit,

Refusing to yield, refusing to quit.

For my children, I rise with the sun;

Every sacrifice made; every battle won;

Their laughter and love fuel my fight

Guiding me through the darkest night.

Brick by brick, I've carved us a new path;

With hope in my heart, I overcame the wrath.

Transforming setbacks; reclaiming what we had;

Finding the strength through the moments that felt sad.

This life I've rebuilt, strong and true,

Is a testament to all we've pushed through.

No matter how steep the climb may be,

I'll keep moving forward for my children fearlessly.

For the future we're building for the love we share,

I'll face every challenge with strength to spare.

The Brave Mask I wore

Each day a façade; a mask I'd wear;
Smiling through pain,
You didn't know was there.
A life full of secrets;
A heart that wouldn't sleep;
I'd laugh when I really wanted to scream and shout;
Hiding the hurt,
While I tried to figure it all out.
Eventually, the mask cracked and shattered,
It fell to the floor,
And in that moment, I couldn't take any more.
I'm done with the pretence;
I'm shedding the guise;
On the rawness of truth,
I will let my soul rise.
No more pretending,
I'm real!
I'm alive!
In the freedom of honesty,
I will finally thrive.

The Journey of Acceptance

As I stand in the broken mirror,
Looking deep into my eyes,
Acknowledging the whole truth behind all the lies,
My past is my canvas,
With colours so bold;
Every shade tells a story,
Brushstrokes unfold.
I finally accept all of who I am,
The scars that I bear;
Each trauma a lesson,
A testament of care.
No more running from shadows that whisper shame;
I embrace my whole self,
A time to reframe.
With every step,
I find my own ground;
In the dance of acceptance,
I find my crown.
I'm learning to love the flaws that I see;
In the acceptance of being me,
I'm finally free.
No need for perfection,
Just a heart that feels true;
I'm becoming the person I always knew.
So here I stand with arms open wide;
In the journey of acceptance,

I'll take it all in my stride.

The Dance of Patience

Healing is a river, slow moving and wide,
With twists and turns, learning to abide.
I won't rush the current;
I won't fight against time;
For patience is wisdom -
A virtue sublime.
Each step on this path is a lesson to learn;
In the ebb and flow,
My heart starts to yearn.
I'll breathe through the moments when doubts start to creep,
Finding strength in the silence,
In the promise to keep.
With every small victory,
I'll celebrate me;
In the garden of healing
I'm planting the seeds that will be.
Growth takes its time;
It's not always clear,
But I trust in the process and conquer my fear,
So, I'll give myself grace;
I'll honour my pace;
In the dance of patience,
I'll find my own space.
With every deep breath,
I'll calm my mind;
In this journey of healing, true peace I will find.

An Illusion of Love

He was everything I thought I wanted,

My type in every way,

A black belt, confidence,

My heart led astray.

A graphic designer with a smile that could charm;

His designs were bright,

But brought visual harm -

Kept glowing like neon,

Yet failed to disarm.

His job was impressive,

But he would make me feel so small,

Like I should be grateful because I'm a nobody after all.

Yet when in need, it would be me who he would ask for cash;

Every promise he made was empty turning into a fleeting flash.

Substances twisted his mind, took him over.

In moments of rage,

I was left behind;

Feeling lower;

In the dim light of Ibiza

I wore my disguise,

Hiding black eyes and bruises beneath sunny skies.

Each mark told a story -

A truth never revealed -

While the world saw a happy couple,

My pain was concealed.

He'd beat me and lash out,

Fuelled by his hype;

As it escalated,

I learnt how to lie.

Our housemate caught him without a mask,

A witness to the scene,

If not for his presence, I'd have faced something more mean;

A dumbbell in hand,

He'd have crossed that line;

In the moments of chaos,

I could no longer be blind.

For nearly two years I thought I was in love,

But the truth of his violence felt like a push and shove;

So I gathered my courage,

Called the police and broke free,

Escaping the chains of his anger,

Reclaiming me.

I chose solitude for three years to heal and find my way,

To rebuild my spirit,

And learn to be ok.

Shattered Reflection

Three years I stood alone,

Learning to be strong,

Healing from the shadows where I felt I belonged.

Then a man entered,

Not my usual type;

His charm mirrored mine,

Pulling me into the hype.

In the beginning he felt like my twin flame;

Every shared secret I felt reassured,

Free of shame.

He became my safe space where I bared my soul,

But little did I know,

He'd take full control.

Love bombing at first,

Sweet words filled the air;

I thought I had found someone who truly did care.

A whirlwind so fast,

I was swept away,

Blinded by the dream,

I didn't see the cracks at play.

What felt like love became a cruel snare;

He took my deepest wounds and left them laid bare.

The trauma I trusted him with,

Became his tool;

Every vulnerability turned into his rule.

He reshaped my truths;

Set traps I couldn't see;

The man I trusted and confided in dismantled me.

The one I once cherished now felt like a ghost,

Tearing apart everything I valued the most.

But I rose up from these ruins,

Reclaimed my faith;

Learnt to love myself,

Before it was too late.

So here's to the journey ahead;

The freedom I gained;

From the depths of deception,

My spirit somehow remained.

No more grand gestures;

No more veils to wear;

I'll stand in my truth,

With my heart laid bare.

Breaking the Cycle

Two paths I walked both lined with pain,
One marked by violence,
The other by blame.
In the first, fists flew; rage uncontained;
A physical prison where love was stained.
The second was more subtle, a whispering ghost;
A master of charm, convincing me the most.
"You're the problem" he said, twisting my mind;
In the web of his words, my truth was left behind.
Each left me shattered, each made me feel frail;
I wore their masks; swallowed their lies;
In the silence of struggle, I lost my own eyes.
Now I stand here, learning to breathe,
Finding my strength in the space to believe,
I need to be single,
To work through my scars;
To untangle the patterns;
To reach for the stars.
Attachment styles woven from trauma and tears;
A journey of healing, confronting my fears;
No more quick fixes; no more running away;
I'll face my reflections; learn to truly stay.
I'm done with the cycle; the trauma and strife,
Claiming my power, embracing my life.
For I deserve peace; I deserve to be whole;
In the process of healing, I'm reclaiming my soul.

Counting on Us

When my world grew colder, I counted on the light;
Three heartbeats beside me, guiding me through the night.
I counted on courage when fear gripped me tight;
In the rhythm of hope, I fought with all my might.
On National Poetry Day, in a national crisis too,
What or who are you counting on? And is anyone counting on you?
Our elders, our women, and those living in poverty's clutch;
The vulnerable among us are counting on us so much!
They're counting on warmth while politician's debate;
While promises are spoken, their delayed action is too late!
Those shivering in the cold, living below the bread line,
Their voices silenced, without a sign;
Their hopes crushed; dreams deferred; longing for a lifeline;
While those in power discuss caps, they're left to freeze;
They leave them wrapped in blankets shivering to their knees.
I refuse to accept a world this unjust,
Where those who built our country are left in the dust;
I'm counting on you - on us - to stand tall,
To break the silence, to answer the call,
Remind the ones in power we will not fall.
They're counting on our silence to soon fade,
While I'm counting on change, on the noise that we've all made!
It's time to stand up, raise our voices so loud!
For the elders who built this country;
For the women whose strength we should celebrate and be proud,
Counting on one another, let's make them proud!

And it's not just those affected by the energy crisis – its women survivors too!

One in five women lose their breath to their ex-partners,

What can we do?!

They're counting on us to break through the chain,

To stand for their safety, to end this pain.

In this national emergency, this is not something that we can delay;

Our hearts must ignite; we cannot look away.

So, I'm counting on you to help me with this fight;

Together we can all stand for what is right!

Let's harness our power, unite for the cause,

To lift the fallen, to rally and applause.

They're counting on us to lead the way,

To push through barriers, come what may.

I'm counting on change and I'm counting on you,

To stand with me side by side, power in numbers pushing through.

They're counting on apathy, on us staying small;

I'm counting on us all to unite to break down the wall!

Politicians, can you hear the call?

Our elders; our women; our poor, they need us all!

Each life matters; each voice is a key;

Together we'll rise; let's set the oppressed free!

Our country is counting on you!

Please it's time to stand tall!

This fight is for us all, no one gets left behind;

It's time for make a change, to be just and kind.

From the vulnerable left in the cold to the cries of the abused;

I'm counting on you, it's time we all refused!

We'll rise together, with our hearts on fire,

Fuelled by passion I'm counting on us all to reach even higher!

Counting Lives, Demanding Justice

I'm counting on fingers as the weeks go by,

Two women a week lose their battle to domestic violence and die.

One hundred and one names Jess Phillips read aloud,

Lives lost to the hands of their abuser; honoured yet still under a shroud.

Counting the children that are in a refuge tonight,

Sixty thousand souls in a tunnel searching for a light.

From the darkness, they run, too young to understand why,

Leaving behind all that they know without a proper goodbye.

In shelters and hostels they find their reprieve,

From homes filled with terror that leaves them no air to breathe.

Counting moments where hearts beat fast;

One in three women bear scars of abuse from their past.

Counting the lives lost in the UK, so far, at the hands of men;

50 women gone, femicide's toll calls for justice again.

One in five women are killed by an ex, even after they leave;

Will there ever be peace? Or just more women to grieve?

If each name, we remember is a pledge to ignite,

The fire in our bellies, to rise up and fight;

Counting on justice, for all victims somewhere, somehow,

To hold abusers accountable, the time is now!

Melodies of Goodbye

I heard the words "Wembley, thank you, goodnight";
The evening air was cool upon my face;
The crowd dispersed beneath the fading light;
Stevie Nicks sang songs of leather and lace.
I tried to say goodbye and sadly failed,
And far away a lonely dog fox wailed.
Melodies linger through heartache and pain,
All crashing down in the mighty landslide;
Feeling freedom; dancing in the rain.
Can I sail through the changing ocean tides?
With whispers of hope I reached for the sky.
So is this "goodnight" or is this "goodbye"?
Longing for connection to soothe the soul;
Saw my reflection in lights of Wembley,
Being rebuilt from broken and not yet whole.
In melodies I learn to be set free;
In this moment - I find where I belong;
Lost in music, answers revealed in song.

Walking at My Own Pace

Today I walked amongst nature`s embrace,
A journey of solitude; walking at my own pace.
Amidst the whispers of the trees and lakes' flow,
I found the sanctuary where my spirit could grow.
They all worry about me and judge,
That I'll be left alone,
On a dusty shelf,
With a heart turned to stone;
But I crave something pure,
Something real and true;
Anything less, well, that could never do.
In the solace of nature, I discover my grace;
Walking at my own pace.
I refuse to settle for something that`s not right -
Only a connection that ignites my light.
A moment to cherish in this tranquil place,
Walking at my own pace.
I'll wait for the one whose heart aligns with mine;
In nature`s company, the grand design;
In this chapter of my story, I'll tell,
Of walks in the woods, where my soul finds its well.
So here I continue to roam,
Hoping that one day I connect with a love that feels like home.

When Lisa first walked into our freedom programme group I just knew she was going to be a wordsmith. She had so much energy and so much to say, but when we've experienced domestic abuse it can be a confusing mess in our head and it can take time to process, express and understand what we've been through. The words are there, just waiting to be released in an orderly fashion and put down on paper. The programmes; our fellow warrior women and our sheer tenacity for justice helps us make sense of our ourselves and enables us to see through the tangled web we were in. Lisa's story, as told through her poetry, is about honouring her resistance, finding the strength which was there all along and rising up using her words to give hope and validation to other survivors. Congratulations Lisa on the publication of your book.

Jacky Mulveen

Project Manager

WE:ARE Women's Empowerment and Recovery Educators

Built from Broken by Lisa Connolly is a poignant and powerful compilation that delves into the raw emotions and experiences of individuals who have faced adversity, particularly in the context of domestic abuse and trauma. The poems are deeply moving, offering a glimpse into the journey of healing, resilience, and self-discovery. Each piece resonates with authenticity and vulnerability, capturing the pain of the past and the strength found in reclaiming one's narrative. The collection skilfully navigates themes of empowerment, hope, and the transformative power of self-expression. Through evocative language and heartfelt verses, the poems shed light on the complexities of survival and the unwavering spirit of those who have endured hardship. Built from Broken is a testament to the human capacity for healing and serves as a source of inspiration for anyone seeking solace and understanding.

Daniel Kay

AccessAbility Arts

DK4 Poetry

Built from Broken the debut poetry collection by Lisa Connolly, invites readers into a nuanced exploration of trauma, resilience, and ultimately, hope. This collection highlights the complexities of abuse, capturing the perspectives of not only those who endure it but also the minds of the abusers – both portrayed through poems, Connolly has constructed in the first person, and the omniscient gaze of an outside observer in her third person pieces.

Each poem resonates with rhythmic energy, weaving catchy rhymes that elevate the gravity of the subject matter while making it accessible. Connolly balances the raw intensity of pain with moments of reflection and healing, offering a multidimensional portrayal of trauma that is both haunting and uplifting, conveying the inner turmoil of the abused with raw honesty.

The poems use vivid imagery, allowing readers to feel the weight of despair and the flickers of hope that emerge. The inclusion of the abuser's perspective adds a chilling layer of complexity, forcing us to confront uncomfortable truths about power dynamics and the cycles of pain. While the poems confront difficult themes head-on, they are infused with a sense of possibility and renewal.

Connolly navigates the landscape of trauma, reminding us that healing is a journey, often marked by small victories and moments of grace.

Mel Wardle Woodend

PhD Student Applied Linguistics, Aston University

Director, Dream Well Writing Ltd

Staffordshire Poet Laureate (2019-2022)

WORD Stafford

Aston Society of Poetry

These are poems which might save your life. They have a universal appeal and speak to the indestructability of the human spirit. The book is a roadmap of being rebuilt from broken whereby the poet records her journey from recovery to empowerment where she rises like a Phoenix from the ashes. Within the narrative is healing for others, love for her children, dancing in the rain to the music of Stevie Nicks and a celebration of National Poetry Day 2024 where she writes a poem that is on point on the theme of counting. Hope whispers and the Phoenix rises in all her glory from the depths of despair. Buy this book. It`s not only a collection of quality writing but inspirational. It might also just save your life.

Ian Henery

Walsall Poet Laureate (2011 - 2016, 2020 – 2021)

The Ian Henery Show

Black Country Xtra

This touching collection is a testament to Connolly's bravery to: confront domestic brutality, dissect the broken pieces, and pave a way for new hope. It's a deeply personal journey to freedom.

Freddie Barker

The Worcestershire Poet Laureate (2024-2025)

Lisa takes us on a tarot reading of a journey underneath a mountain, from light to light. Her motherly words are a guiding hand through the darkness, ending with a rallying cry for unity.

Her poetry, whilst overflowing with humanity, love and compassion, also tells the stark truth of an open heart. Whilst avoiding the thrills and shock value of a horror story, she describes horrific situations plainly and simply as they are. Lisa has a natural poetic rhythm in her voice but also highlights, with clarity, the bridges between safety and danger and how easy it is to blindly cross these. Her words are both warning and healing and she emerges with a mission to save the world.

A truly inspiring voice that must be heard as loud and in as many places, as possible!

Laura Liptrot

Actor, poet and playwright

Rosetta Theatre

Built from Broken by Lisa Connolly is so much more than a traditional book of poetry. It is an incredibly moving and inspiring account of one woman's journey through abuse, control, surviving, and ultimately thriving. However, this collection is more than one woman's story, it is a rallying cry for social change and better protection for the vulnerable. I devoured this poetry in one sitting, on an emotional rollercoaster driven by the flowing rhythms and clever imagery laced throughout these poems. 'Built from Broken' is not only a brilliant poetry book, it is an important one. A book that could change lives, a book that could change the world, and a book I am very grateful to have read.

Jade Hartley

Actor, poet and playwright

Rosetta Theatre

Built from Broken by Lisa Connolly is a profoundly moving collection that explores the journey from trauma to healing with incredible depth and grace. Every poem in this compilation is as compelling as the next, capturing the raw emotion, strength, and resilience of those who have faced adversity. Connolly's evocative language brings these stories to life, allowing readers to feel the pain, hope, and empowerment that radiates through each verse.

This collection isn't just a reflection of survival—it's a testament to the indomitable spirit that rises from hardship. Every line resonates with authenticity, providing solace and inspiration to those seeking to reclaim their narrative. Built from Broken is a powerful reminder of the human capacity for healing and a must-read for anyone looking for a source of strength and understanding.

Diyodi Menon

Project Manager

Built from broken by Lisa Connolly is one of the most powerful debut collections I have had the honour to read. The subject matter is discussed with raw honesty and emotion, pulling the frayed threads of a bruised soul together into a tapestry of survival, showing Lisa's empathy for those who have also survived the abyss of abuse, and support for those who may feel alone in their lives. This collection is a shining example of the power of poetry to illuminate the important issues of society. Lisa is to be commended for both her bravery and strength in creating this collection; Counting Lives, Demanding Justice is not an easy call to hear, but one that deserves to be repeated until society changes attitudes. Thank you, Lisa, from all the women whose voices you have helped raise.

Leena Batchelor

Worcestershire Poet Laureate (2020 – 2021)

Owner Script Haven, Worcester`s premier independent bookshop and cafe

Pixie Muse Poetry

In Built From Broken the poet masterfully captures the intricate dance of healing, self-care, and resilience. Each verse resonates with authenticity, revealing the profound connection between helping others and nurturing oneself.

The collection radiates empowerment, encouraging readers to tap into their own inner strength and limitless potential. The imagery is vivid and uplifting, inviting us to bask in the light of our own capabilities.

However, these poems are not just a reflection of personal experiences; they serve as a guiding light for anyone on a path of healing. With its blend of hope and truth, Built From Broken inspires us all to embrace our journeys and remember that healing is a shared experience—one that brings us closer to understanding both ourselves and others. A truly inspiring read!

Scarlett Ward

Staffordshire Poet Laureate (2024 – 2025)

Founder of Fawn Press

Whenever I'm asked to review a new poetry collection I tend to view the content with an individual, piece by piece approach, each piece a stand-alone testament to poetic ideals. In the case of Built From Broken I feel to do that would remove the sense of purpose of the book; its contents and the author's desire to metaphorically take our hand and lead us along a thorny path of relationships and, in this case, the personal abuse that can exist within them.

The book opens with poetic counselling, meditation and analysis before we enter a world of uncertainty, disbelief and fading hope that things will improve or, worse still, believing we are the author of our own demise. At times, darkness is banished only to present itself from a forgotten shadow left cast in the corner.

In the darkened room of fear that lies between the covers of this collection we are given shafts of light to encourage us to complete our collective mental and emotional voyage. Hope and light do intensify and win over in the forms of personal freedom and renewed, revitalised strength and purpose of a survivor.

The poems, or chapters as they appear to be, are represented by a continuous, sinuous ribbon of barbed wire snags. The more you struggle, the more entangled you become. At the turning point in this work, freedom and tenacity win the day, building a new life.

Powerful, insightful, heart-breaking and empowering for all victims of abuse. For those who haven't witnessed abuse, read on. You never know what nightmares exist behind a smile.

Buy this book and be enlightened!

Brendan Hawthorne

Wednesbury Poet Laureate (2014 – 2016)

Award Winning Poet, Playwright and Author

Lisa Connolly's new poetry collection is a raw and heartfelt exploration of personal healing, trauma, and empowerment. Her work moves fluidly between themes of emotional strength, self-discovery, and the aftermath of toxic relationships, offering readers a deeply reflective and relatable experience. Poems like The Healing Healer highlight the importance of self-care even for those who help others, while pieces such as When the Love Bombing Ends and Narcissistic Fog poignantly depict the emotional toll of abusive relationships. Connolly masterfully combines a therapeutic approach with powerful imagery, guiding readers through pain, resilience, and ultimately hope.

Her poems often capture moments of self-realisation, as seen in Save Yourself and Built from Broken, where she challenges societal narratives and encourages women to reclaim their power. The rhythm of her writing, though simple, is rich in emotion, drawing readers into the internal worlds of her narrators. In particular, her ability to reflect the unseen battles of trauma survivors is both moving and enlightening, as in Too Scared to Sleep and Triggered.

Connolly's work feels like a personal conversation with each reader, offering solidarity and validation for those who have experienced similar struggles. The collection does not shy away from difficult truths, yet it is infused with hope, as shown in Freedom and Fresh Start. It's a poignant reminder that healing, though not linear, is possible. For anyone seeking poetry that speaks directly to the human spirit's capacity for renewal, Connolly's collection is a must-read.

Katie Victoria

Actor, poet and playwright

Rosetta Theatre

‘Built from Broken’ by Lisa Connolly is a whirlwind adventure through the devastation caused by a relationship which encounters domestic violence and abuse. The beginnings of a relationship, the stronghold of violence and then finally the movement into survivorship. The author manages to channel their emotions and pass them onto the reader. The reader then encounters the journey, albeit in physical safety. Raw emotion throughout, a must read to ensure that the voice of survival is never lost.

Dr Lucy Kelsall-Knight – University of Birmingham

Lisa Connolly's Built from Broken is unwaveringly direct and often painfully raw and honest. Reflecting on the change of self in the aftermath of experiencing domestic violence, the author gives an unfiltered look at fear, confusion, and trauma, bringing the reader on the path to healing. With its rhymes demanding to be heard, the collection provides validation to survivors and makes a powerful contribution to contemporary poetry.

Dr Polina Gavin - Aston Poetry Society, Aston University

Built From Broken is a book that feels like sitting down with a friend opening up about their toughest battles, showing both the raw pain and the hard-won resilience that follow. With each poem, you get a glimpse into the journey of someone who's been through trauma and emotional difficulties but has come out on the other side. It made me feel seen.

Something I really liked was the author's honesty and vulnerability. I found poems that highlighted the importance of self-care and self-reflection, even when caring for others.

Many of the poems dive into the reality of abusive relationships in a way that's both relatable and eye-opening. They pull you into an emotional rollercoaster of feeling trapped, manipulated, and lost. However, it also shines a light on the courage it takes to leave an abusive relationship.

As you read the book, you feel the shift from pain to empowerment, like walking alongside someone learning to find joy again.

What I love is how the collection celebrates the power of community and sisterhood. I felt like there was the feeling of "you're not alone", making it easy" to connect with the poems, even if you're new to poetry.

Ultimately, Built From Broken is about rebuilding yourself, bit by bit. It's a beautiful read for anyone who's ever had to pick up their pieces after experiencing hardship.

Andrea Gardia - Writer and Poet

www.ingramcontent.com/pod-product-compliance
Lightning Source LLC
LaVergne TN
LVHW052009160826
845678LV00005B/1696

* 9 7 8 1 0 3 6 9 0 4 5 2 4 *